British History

H.C DILSTON

All rights reserved. © H.C Dilston

ISBN: 978-0-244-93528-3

2017

The British Isles has a marvellous and fascinating history going back thousands of years. This quiz has questions from many different periods, starting with Ancient Britain and ending in Post war Britain. It doesn't claim to feature every important aspect of British history, but does include many. Some questions are more obscure than others, but there is multiple choice options to allow for educated guesses. Many of the answers have more information relating to the question.

Questions

Ancient Britain

1. What did British tribes use woad for?
a. Dying skin blue b. Starting fires c. Seasoning meat d. Rope

2. Skara Brae is Europe's most complete Neolithic village, and is a UNESCO World Heritage site. Where in Scotland is it located?
a. Skye b. Orkneys c. Shetland Isles d. Arran

3. What is the name given to a typical house made during the Bronze and Iron Age?

4. Which of the following was the celebration of summer solstice?
a. Yule b. Litha c. Ostara d. Mabon

5. Approximately how many years old is Stonehenge?
a. 3,000 b. 4,000 c. 5,000 d. 10,000

6. Which is Europe's largest Iron Age hillfort?

a. Maiden Castle b. Winterbourne Poor Lot Barrows c. Old Oswestry Hill Fort d. Uffington Castle

7. What came first the Bronze or Iron age?

8. What were the religious leaders of Iron age Britain known as?

9. What is 'Old Sarum'?

a. Burial mound b. Hill fort c. Iron Age road d. Treasure hoard

10. Which tree was considered sacred by the ancient Britons?

a. Birch b. Sycamore c. Maple d. Yew

Roman

1. What year did Julius Caesar and the Romans first invade Britain?

a. 150 B.C b. 55 B.C c. 23 A.D d. 75 A.D

2. Boudica was queen of which Brittonic tribe that rebelled against Roman rule?

a. Brigantes b. Regni c. Trinovantes d. Iceni

3. What is the name of the wall, the Romans built north of Hadrian's Wall, that stretched across what is now known as the Central Belt of Scotland, the area the stretches from Edinburgh in the east, to Glasgow in the west?

4. Camulodunum was once the capital of the Roman province of Britannia. What is the name of the town now?

a. Colchester b. Salisbury c. Norwich d. Dover

5. What was the name of the Gallo-Roman general responsible for much of the Roman conquest of Britain?

6. Dere and Watling are names of two old Roman what?

a. Roads b. Coins c. Towns d. Temples

7. How many Roman soldiers were garrisoned on Emperor Hadrian's Wall at the end of his reign, A.D 138?

a. 3,000 b. 10,000 c. 40,000 d. 60,000

8. How long was Hadrian's Wall?

a. 25 miles b. 49 miles c. 64 miles d. 73 miles

9. What animal did the Romans introduce to Britain?

a. Rabbit b. Goose c. Squirrel d. Rat

10. What century did the Roman province of Britannia come to an end?

a. 2nd century b. 3rd century c. 4th century d. 5th century

Anglo Saxon

1. Who wrote Historia ecclesiastica gentis Anglorum, The Ecclesiastical History of the English People?

a. St Bede b. St Aidan c. St Cuthbert d. St Augustine

2. In 1939 an Anglo Saxon ship burial was excavated, at Sutton Hoo. It was one of the greatest ever finds of treasure within the British Isles. Which Anglo Saxon Kingdom is the site located?

a. East Anglia b. Kent c. Mercia d. Northumbria

3. After seeing them for the first time, who thought the Anglo Saxons should be co-heirs of the angels of heaven?

a. Julius Caesar b. Pope Gregory I c. Queen Boudica d. Emperor Hadrian

4. Who was the last Anglo Saxon king of England?

5. What year were the Anglo Saxon kingdoms united to create the Kingdom of England?

a. 603 A.D b. 764 A.D c. 927 A.D d. 1066 A.D

6. What happened to the monastery on the island of Lindisfarne, where the Lindisfarne Gospels were made, in 793 A.D?

a. Swept away during a storm b. Plague killed all the monks c. Attacked by Vikings d. Foundations were laid.

7. Which one of the following is not a female Anglo Saxon name?

a. Edith b. Mildred c. Alice d. Hilda

8. Who became the first Archbishop of Canterbury in 597 A.D?

9. Where was Beowulf, an epic Anglo Saxon poem about a monster attacking a Mead Hall, set?

a. England b. Scandinavia c. Valhalla d. Middle Earth

10. King Alfred the Great was crowned King of Wessex aged 21. Where was his capital?

a. Winchester b. Canterbury c. Hastings d. Salisbury

Viking

1. What was the area of England the Vikings controlled known as?

2. Which modern UK city was known as Jorvik during the Viking era?

3. What was Odin?

a. Dragon b. Prince c. God d. Warrior

4. What are Viking symbols known as?

5. Thor is a Norse god associated with?

a. Thunder b. Sea c. Fire d. Ice

6. Aelle, King of Northumbria was captured and blood eagled by the Vikings. What was this?

a. Thrown off a cliff b. Entrails fed to an Eagle c. Hung from a tree and sliced in two. d. Eagle carved into the back then ribs and lungs removed.

7. What percentage of Shetland place names are of Viking origin?

a. 19% b. 56% c. 75% d. 95%

8. A few weeks before King Harold and his army faced the invading Normans at the Battle of Hastings they beat Norwegian Vikings at which battle?

9. Where was King Canute / Cnut born?

a. England b. Norway c. Denmark d. Sweden

10. During the time Vikings were raiding and settling on the British Isles, the Vikings reached Greenland and Iceland. Did they reach North America?

High to Late Middle Ages

1. Who was murdered in Canterbury Cathedral in 1170?

2. In 1290 King Edward I issued an edict demanding what?

a. Tax on windows b. Expulsion of Jews from England c. Closing of monasteries d. War on France

3. Which part of the UK was first to report deaths due to Bubonic Plague, at the start of the Black Death in 1348?

a. South East England b. East Anglia c. Wales d. South West England

4. What did Wat Tyler lead in 1381?

5. Who was King Richard the Lionheart's adversary during the Third Crusade?

6. Which of the following was not one of Robin Hood's Merry Men?

a. Little John b. Thomas the archer c. Will Scarlet d. Much the Miller's Son

7. Who was victorious at the Battle of Bannockburn in 1314?

8. What famous battle between the English and French took place on St Crispin's Day?

9. Who led an uprising against the English in Wales in 1400, and was the last native Welsh, Prince of Wales?

10. Who was the first person to print books in English and published Chaucer's Canterbury Tales?

Tudor

1. What relation is Queen Elizabeth I to Queen Elizabeth II, who became queen in 1952?

a. 14th Great Grandmother b. 1st Cousin - 13 times removed c. 15th Great Aunt d. No relation.

2. What is the name of the shipwreck that was discovered in 1971, in the Solent, and was recovered for restoration in 1982, that was part of King Henry VIII's navy?

3. What was William Shakespeare's father's occupation?

a. Leather & wool dealer b. Farmer c. Butcher d. Thatcher

4. What is Virginia Dare famous for?

a. King Henry VIII's mistress b. Queen Elizabeth I's Lady in Waiting c. White Witch d. First English baby to be born in the American colonies

5. What was Francis Drake, Vice Admiral of the English fleet, doing at Plymouth Hoe, shortly before the battle against the Spanish Armada, in 1588?

a. Playing cards b. Horse riding c. Getting his hair cut d. Playing bowls

6. What was the estimated population of London during the Elizabethan age?

a. 200,000 b. 400,000 c. 800,000 d. 1 million

7. What was the name of the 1586 plot that aimed to assassinate protestant Queen Elizabeth and put her cousin, Mary Queen of Scots, who was Catholic, on the throne?

8. Who was King Henry VIII's first wife?

a. Catherine of Aragon b. Anne of Cleves c. Anne Boleyn d. Jane Seymour

9. What English / Scottish battle that took place in 1513, does the Scottish pipe tune, Flowers of the Forest commemorate?

10. How old was Edward VI when he became King?

a. 9 b. 14 c. 18 d. 23

Stuart

1. Which scientist discovered, in 1672, that white light was made up of a range of colours?

2. What was the street called, where the Great Fire of London began in 1666?
a. Cake Walk b. Pie Street c. Apple Mews d. Pudding Lane

3. Samuel Pepys wrote a famous diary about life in London. Where did he work during this time?
a. Westminster Abbey b. Navy Board c. East India Company d. Palace of Whitehall

4. Which part of Britain was the self-styled 'Witchfinder General' Matthew Hopkins most prolific in his 'witch hunting'?
a. Cornwall b. East Anglia c. Midlands d. Scottish Highlands

5. Who supported Oliver Cromwell during the English Civil War; Cavaliers or Roundheads?

6. Which Stuart monarch has a style of architecture named after them, that became popular again in the late Victorian era?

7. The English Civil War was part of a greater conflict. What was this war known as?

8. Guy Fawkes was in charge of guarding the gunpowder below the House of Lords, but who led the plot to assassinate protestant King James, during the state opening of Parliament?

a. Thomas Wintour b. Thomas Percy c. John Wright d. Robert Catesby

9. Jethro Tull invented what in 1701?

a. Reflecting Telescope b. Seed Drill c. Pocket Watch d. Steam Engine

10. King Charles granted a Flemish painter in 1638, denizenship, which was an early form of permanent residency. The painter had done various portraits of the royal family and aristocracy. Who was it?

Georgian

1. Why was Charles Dickens's father imprisoned, when Charles was a 12 year old boy in 1824?

a. debt b. illegal gambling c. fraud d. blasphemy

2. Which country did poet Lord Byron travel to, so he could assist in their fight for independence?

a. Portugal b. Serbia c. Italy d. Greece

3. Which famous female author, of the Georgian era, was not well known during her lifetime, as her books were published anonymously?

4. The Royal Pavilion was re-designed by architect John Nash between 1815 and 1822, as a residence for King George IV in which English seaside town?

a. Eastbourne b. Newquay c. Bournemouth d. Brighton

5. Who was the first ever United Kingdom Prime Minister, in power between 1721 - 1742?

a. Spencer Compton b. Robert Walpole c. Henry Pelham d. William Cavendish

6. What was the name of the main opposition party to the Tory Party in the Georgian era?

7. What did Admiral Horatio Nelson suffer from?

a. Seasickness b. Fear of heights c. Arthritis d. Deafness

8. Prussia, Netherlands and Hanover were allies with Britain in which famous battle?

9. The Georgian era is named after the four King Georges of the era. King George I, II, III and IV were all part of which royal house?

a. Orange b. Regent c. Saxon d. Hanover

10. Royal Crescent is considered one of the finest Georgian streets in the UK and is grade 1 listed. Which city is it in?

a. Liverpool b. London c. Edinburgh d. Bath

Victorian

1. How old was Queen Victoria, when she died?
a. 67 b. 78 c. 81 d. 88

2. Crimean War nurse Florence Nightingale became known as?
a. Angel of Mercy b. Crimean Saviour c. Lady of Hope d. Lady with the Lamp

3. Michael Faraday is considered a founder of what type of science?
a. Electrochemistry b. Zoology c. Genetics d. Oncology

4. There was 12 teams in the world's first ever football league, in England. The first season was 1888/89. Who won the league?
a. Aston Villa b. Everton c. Notts County d. Preston North End

5. Isambard Kingdom Brunel created an extension of the Great Western Railway, of which he was Chief Engineer, from Exeter towards Plymouth. Instead of using steam locomotives, what did he use to power the trains?

a. Electricity b. Water pumps c. Wind d. Vacuum traction

6. The Condition and Treatment of the Children employed in the Mines and Colliers of the United Kingdom was a report made for the British Parliament in 1842. What was the ages of the youngest workers it found evidence of working down coal mines?

a. 4 and 5 b. 6 and 7 c. 8 and 9 d. 10 and 11

7. What did Alexander Graham Bell receive a patent for in 1876?

a. Telephone b. Air Conditioner c. Audiometer d. Metal Detector

8. During the Victorian era, Ireland was part of the United Kingdom. Between 1845 and 1852 there was a devastating famine, after the failure of what type of crop?

a. Wheat b. Oats c. Barley d. Potatoes

9. Which city became the first in the world to have a street lit up using electric incandescent light bulbs?

a. London b. Manchester c. Oxford d. Newcastle upon Tyne

10. What was the name of the ship that Charles Darwin travelled on, during his scientific expeditions. HMS?

a. Beagle b. Dolphin c. Terrier d. Otter

Edwardian

1. In which city was The RMS Titanic built?

a. Southampton b. Belfast c. Glasgow d. Sunderland

2. Which political party won a landslide election victory in 1906?

a. Labour b. Conservatives c. Whigs d. Liberals

3. Who was the Suffragette that leaped in front of the King's race horse?

a. Emily Davison b. Emmeline Pankhurst c. Teresa Billington-Greig d. Janie Allen

4. Which city is associated with Art Nouveau architect, Charles Rennie Mackintosh?

a. Belfast b. Manchester c. Edinburgh d. Glasgow

5. In 1909, what did Louis Bleriot do?

a. Flew across the English Channel b. Piloted the first passenger flight c. Crashed a plane in the garden of Buckingham Palace d. Broke the flight speed record

6. Which famous children's character, created by writer J.M Barrie, first appeared on stage in 1904?

7. Which renowned Edwardian music composer grew up in the Malvern Hills, Worcestershire?

8. King Edward, who the era was named after, was the?

a. I (1st) b. III (3rd) c. IV (4th) d. VII (7th)

9. Which country won the most gold medals, at the London Olympics of 1908?

a. Great Britain b. U.S.A c. Sweden d. France

10. Who came third in the 1910 UK General Election? The Liberals won, with 272 seats.

a. Conservatives b. Irish Parliamentary Party c. Labour d. Social Democratic Federation

World War One

1. How many British soldiers were killed on the first day of the Battle of the Somme, 1st July 1916?

a. 4,800 b. 10,345 c. 15,001 d. 19,200

2. Which world famous female author was a Red Cross nurse during WWI?

3. Who wrote the World War One poem, In Flanders Fields?

a. John McCrae b. Wilfred Owen c. Siegfried Sassoon d. Rupert Brooke

4. There was two UK prime ministers during WW1, David Lloyd George was one, who was the other?

5. The Royal Air Force was founded on 1st April 1918, with just over seven months of the war remaining. What was the aviation section of the army known as, before the RAF was created?

6. What happened to Field Marshal Horatio Herbert Kitchener, who was Secretary of State for War and organised Britain's largest ever volunteer army?

a. Shot on the Western Front b. Died of Malaria in Palestine c. Bi plane crashed d. Killed when the ship he was on hit a mine

7. Who was the last ever surviving Tommy, who fought in the trenches?

8. What was the name of the German airships that dropped bombs on the UK?

9. Who had the highest number of casualties as a result of the naval Battle of Jutland? Germany or Great Britain?

10. Which one of the following UK Prime Ministers was not a WW1 veteran?

a. Alec Douglas-Home b. Harold McMillan c. Clement Atlee d. Anthony Eden

Inter War Years

1. Labour won their first UK General Election in 1924. Who was the first Labour Prime Minister?

a. Keir Hardie b. Arthur Henderson c. Philip Snowden d. Ramsey McDonald

2. In 1935, Mr Beere became the first British person ever, to do what?

a. Buy a TV license b. Swim the English Channel c. Water Ski d. Pass the driving test

3. Who discovered Penicillin in 1928?

4. A historic event took place at Alexandra Palace, London on the 2nd November, 1936. What was it?

5. Which northern town was the starting point for a march to London, in 1936, to protest about high unemployment?

a. Wigan b. Grimsby c. Redcar d. Jarrow

6. In 1930, Amy Johnson was the first ever female pilot to fly alone to?

a. Australia b. USA c. Canada d. France

7. Fred Perry first started playing tennis on public courts near the housing estate, where he lived. How many times did he win the Wimbledon Men's Single Championship?

a. Once b. Twice c. Three times d. Four times

8. Which famous London born actor, directed and starred in his first feature length film, The Kid, in 1921?

9. Who led the British Union of Fascists, in the 1930s?

10. King Edward VIII abdicated in 1936, when he married American divorcee, Wallis Simpson. His brother became King George VI, but what was his real first name, that he was known as before his accession?

a. Henry b. Albert c. William d. David

Empire

1. What was the cause of Lawrence of Arabia's death?

a. Malaria b. Motorbike accident c. Air raid d. Shot by enemy

2. What year did Australia become independent?

a. 1788 b. 1901 c. 1825 d.1934

3. What was Belize called before it became independent?

a. British Central America b Victoria c. British Mexico d. British Honduras

4. What city was the summer capital of India during the British Raj?

a. Bombay b. Shimla c. Delhi d. Karachi

5. In 1920, the British Empire was at its largest. At that time, what percentage of Earth's land mass was part of the empire?

a. 7.6% b. 16.7% c. 23.8% d. 41.6%

6. Which island/s in the Pacific Ocean, remains under British sovereignty & jurisdiction, as a British Overseas Territory?

a. Pitcairn Islands b. New Britain c. Cook Islands d. South Island

7. Between 1953 and 1963 the British made a new Federation of Rhodesia and Nyasaland, also known as the Central African Federation (CAF), that was semi-independent. Which of the following modern era countries was not part of it?

a. Zambia b. Zimbabwe c. Botswana d. Malawi

8. What does a waterfall and lake in Africa have in common with a city in British Columbia, Canada and a hill near the city of Wellington, New Zealand?

9. What is the name of the famous luxury hotel in Singapore, which is named after the founder of the city state?

10. The Happy Valley set were white British settlers that became known for their decadence and party lifestyle in the years between WWI and WWII. What part of the Empire were they from?

a. Kenya b. Hong Kong c. Jamaica d. South Africa

World War Two

1. Which cathedral was destroyed during the Blitz?

a. St Paul's - London b. The Cathedral Church of St Peter and St Paul - Sheffield c. St Michael's - Coventry d. The Cathedral Church of St Thomas of Canterbury - Portsmouth

2. Which Nordic country did British troops arrive at, in April 1940, to help resist the German invasion?

a. Norway b. Denmark c. Sweden d. Finland

3. What was the name of the secret base where the Enigma code was cracked, that enabled the Allies to read German messages?

4. What was the official name of 'Dad's Army'?

5. Which one of the following beaches did British troops land on, on the 6th June, 1944, D-Day?

a. Omaha b. Utah c. Juno d. Gold

6. Douglas Bader was a Spitfire ace and Battle of Britain hero. What disability did he have, when he flew his plane during the aerial battles?

a. No hearing b. One arm c. One eye d. No legs

7. What was the name of the Royal Navy ship that was sunk by the Bismark on the 24th May, 1941?

8. After the war some veterans joined the 'Goldfish Club'. What was the requirement of membership?

a. Submariner b. To have survived a torpedo hitting a ship c. Took part in an attack on a German ship or U Boat aboard a small Motor Torpedo Boat d. An airman that parachuted or crash landed into the sea

9. What regiment of the Armed Forces did David Stirling create, in the desert of North Africa, in 1941?

10. Who invented the bouncing bombs that the Dambusters used during their famous attack on Germany's dams?

Post War

1. Who was the Health Secretary when the NHS was founded in 1948?

2. What was the name of the ship that is seen as the beginning of mass non-white immigration to Britain, that docked in 1948?

3. Who did England beat in the Semi Final of the 1966 World Cup to reach the final, where they beat West Germany, 4-2?

a. Soviet Union b. Mexico c. Portugal d. Uruguay

4. Was the 1975 referendum to decide whether the UK should?

a. Join the European Community b. Remain a member of the European Community

5. Where was Princess Elizabeth when she succeeded to the throne, after her father, King George VI, died?

a. South Africa b. Rhodesia c. Kenya d. Canada

6. What was the top speed of the Concorde?

a. 900 mph b. 1,005 mph c. 1,354 mph d. 2,000 mph

7. What is the name used to describe the conflict in Northern Ireland, that lasted from the late 1960s until the peace agreement in 1998?

8. Which one of the following was one of the new towns that were created following The New Towns Act 1946?

a. Welwyn Garden City b. Letchworth c. Stevenage d. Hertford

9. Before settling on just The Beatles, what did the band call themselves?

a. Silver Beatles b. Ruby Beatles c. Gold Beatles d. Iron Beatles

10. In 1980 the SAS stormed the embassy of which country, to end a violent hostage situation?

a. Saudi Arabia b. Kuwait c. Iran d. Iraq

Who Said What

1. "England expects that every man will do his duty."

a. Admiral Nelson b. Duke of Wellington c. Winston Churchill d. Earl Haig

2. "I know I have the body but of a weak and feeble woman; but I have the heart and stomach of a king, and of a king of England too"

a. Queen Victoria b. Queen Anne c. Queen Elizabeth I d. Queen Mary

3. "Dr Livingstone, I Presume?"

a. Rudyard Kipling b. Henry Morton Stanley c. Cecil Rhodes d. John Hanning Speke

4. "Germany does not want war. Hitler does not want war. He is a most remarkable personality, one of the greatest I have ever met in the whole of my life, and I have met some very great men."

a. Oswald Moseley b. Lord Rothermere c. Captain Archibald Ramsey M.P d. David Lloyd George

5. "I love peace and quiet, I hate politics and turmoil. We women are not made for governing, and if we are good women, we must dislike these masculine occupations."

a. Queen Victoria b. Dame Barbara Cartland c. Queen Mary d. Florence Nightingale

6. "I have found it impossible to carry the heavy burden of responsibility and to discharge my duties as King, as I would wish to do without the help and support of the woman I love."

a. King George IV b. King Edward VIII c. King Edward VII d. King George V

7. "The British nation is unique in this respect: they are the only people who like to be told how bad things are, who like to be told the worst."

a. Margaret Thatcher b. King George III c. H.H Asquith d. Winston Churchill

8. "In a time of universal deceit, telling the truth is a revolutionary act."

a. George Orwell b. Oscar Wilde c. Wilfred Owen d. Kim Philby

9. "So enormous, so dreadful, so irremediable did the slave trade's wickedness appear that my own mind was completely made up for abolition."

a. William Pitt b. Benjamin Disraeli c. Charles Dickens d. William Wilberforce

10. "Carry out a random act of kindness, with no expectation of reward, safe in the knowledge that one day someone might do the same for you."

a. John Lennon b. Enid Blyton c. Princess Diana d. Roald Dahl

Answers

Ancient Britain

1. a. Dying skin blue. Woad is a natural plant dye.

2. b. Orkneys. The settlement was occupied from approximately 3180 BC to about 2500 BC.

3. Roundhouse. They were made of stone or of wooden posts joined by wattle-and-daub panels and a conical thatched roof.

4. b. Litha. Yule - winter solstice, Ostara - spring equinox, Mabon - autumn equinox

5. It is estimated that construction of Stonehenge began in 3,100 B.C

6. 6. a. Maiden Castle. Located in Dorset, this vast fort has multiple high ramparts. Winterbourne Poor Lot

Barrows is a collection of burial mounds in the same county. Old Oswestry Hill Fort is another large Iron Age fort, and is in Shropshire, near the Welsh border. It is thought to have been the home of an Iron Age tribe. Uffington Castle, in Oxfordshire, is at the summit of Whitehorse Hill, near The White Horse, a large chalk cut hill figure that is 110m / 360ft long and considered to be about 3000 years old.

7. The Bronze Age. It refers to the type of metal that was smelted to make tools and weapons. Bronze is created by combining copper and tin. Iron is extracted from rock or ore, and never found in its pure elemental state. One big advantage of iron is that it can be sharpened.

8. Druids. They were the priest class of the pagan religion.

9. b. Hill fort. Located on a hill about 2 miles (3 km) north of modern Salisbury, Wiltshire.

10. d. Yew. Evergreen, they signified rebirth and immortality. Some Yews in Britain are estimated to be 4,000 years old, which means they were growing at the time of ancient Druids.

Roman

1. b. 55 B.C. He took with him two Roman legions. After winning some battles against the Celtic tribes (Britons) in south-east England he went back to France.

2. d. Iceni. She led a revolt in 60 or 61 A.D as Queen of the Iceni, and from her chariot led Britons in successfully destroying major Roman settlements, before the Romans rallied and she was then defeated.

3. Antonine Wall. It was 39 miles long and made of wood and earth mounds, with a deep ditch on the northern side. Unlike Hadrian's Wall, very little of it can still be seen today.

4. a. Colchester. The town had a senate house, an amphitheatre (with seating for up to 5000 people) and a Roman chariot racing circus, as well as temples and manufacturers making pottery, glass etc.

5. Agricola / Gnaeus Julius Agricola. He was made consul and governor of Britannia in 77 A.D. Most of what is known about him comes from the Roman historian, Tacitus, who was his son in law.

6. a. Roads. 'Dere Street' goes from York to the Antonine Wall, and 'Watling Street' was a paved route from Dover to Wroxeter. Neither of the names were used during the Roman era, but derive from Old English.

7. b. 10,000. There was a total of 15 forts along the length of the wall.

8. d. 73 miles. It stretches from Bowness on Solway in the west, to Wallsend on Tyne, in the suburbs of Newcastle, in the east.

9. a. Rabbit. In 2005 an archaeological dig in Norfolk uncovered the remains of a 2,000-year-old rabbit. It is believed that legions brought rabbits from Spain, where they were reared in walled enclosures and then used for meat.

10. d. 5th century. 410. A.D. Rome was under siege from the Visigoths and no forces could be wasted by staying in remote Britain.

Anglo Saxon

1. St Bede. The work was completed in 731 A.D at his monastery in Jarrow, Northumbria.

2. a. East Anglia. The site is near Woodbridge in Suffolk. It is a National Trust property, open to the public. Much of the Sutton Hoo treasure, including the iconic Anglo Saxon helmet, is displayed in the British Museum in London.

3. b. Pope Gregory I. In Rome he came across some Angle children in a slave market. He asked who they were and was told they were called "Anglii" (Angles), he replied with a Latin pun that translates well into English: "Bene, nam et angelicam habent faciem, et tales angelorum in caelis decet esse coheredes" "It is well, for they have an angelic face, and such people ought to be co-heirs of the angels in heaven."

4. King Harold / King Harold Godwinson. He became King in January 1066, and was killed during the Battle of Hastings, against the invading Normans, on the 14th October, 1066.

5. c. 927 A.D by King Æthelstan.

6. c. Attacked by Vikings. It was one of the earliest raids on Britain, and heralded the beginning of the Viking era. St Bede wrote, "On the sixth day, before the ides of January in the same year, the harrowing inroads of heathen men made lamentable havoc in the church of God in Holy-island, by rapine and slaughter."

7. c. Alice. Alice was a French Norman name, the other three being Anglo Saxon. Norman names became popular after 1066, and still remain more popular today than those of Anglo Saxon origin.

8. Augustine. He was a Benedictine monk from Rome, and he was chosen by Pope Gregory the Great to lead a mission to Britain to baptise King Æthelberht of Kent, who had married a French Christian princess, Bertha. He is considered the founder of the English church and 'apostle to the English'.

9. b. Scandinavia. Beowulf, a hero of Geatland (now Gotaland in southern Sweden) assists Hrothgar, the king of the Danes.

10. a. Winchester.

Viking

1. Dane law. The area was the eastern part of England.

2. York. There is a large visitor attraction in York, all about when Vikings ruled the city.

3. c. God. The All Father of all the Norse gods. His eldest son is Thor.

4. Runes. They are the letters in Germanic alphabets that were used before the adoption of the Latin alphabet

5. a. Thunder. Thursday is named after Thor. Thors day.

6. d. Eagle carved into the back, then ribs and lungs removed.

7. d. 95%. Shetland was part of Norway until the 15th Century.

8. Battle of Stamford Bridge. The battle took place in the East Riding of Yorkshire. Approximately 9,000 Norwegian Vikings clashed with 15,000 English. Harald Hardrada who led the Norwegians was killed by an arrow to his windpipe and they suffered a heavy defeat . Tostig Godwinson, Earl of Northumbria, brother of Harald of England and his rebels fought alongside the Norwegians. He had been exiled when Harald was adviser to King Edward the Confessor, and he then convinced Harald Hardrada of Norway to invade.

9. c. Denmark. He was born in Denmark, 995 A.D, and became King of England, Denmark, Norway and part of Sweden. He died in 1035 and is buried in Winchester.

10. Yes. They crossed the Atlantic in approximately 1000 A.D. In 1960 a Viking settlement was discovered at L'Anse aux Meadows, by husband and wife, Helge

Ingstad and Anne Stine Ingstad, from Norway. This crossing was 500 years before Christopher Columbus sailed to the New World!

High to Late Middle Ages

1. Thomas Becket. He was Archbishop of Canterbury from 1162 until his death. He was killed by supporters of King Henry II, who he was in dispute with over church powers. Pope Alexander III canonised him in 1173, and is now known as Saint Thomas of Canterbury.

2. b. Expulsion of Jews from England. They were banished for over 360 years, and were only allowed to move to England when Oliver Cromwell took power in 1657. Fifteen years before the expulsion, King Edward I created the Statute of Jewry which had banned usury (money lending for interest), and debtors of Jews were no longer liable to pay debts. They could not live outside certain towns and cities and had to wear yellow felt badges on their clothing. There was an estimated 2000 or so living in England at the time. They were allowed to work in other trades, but the edict came into force when it was found many were still practicing usury secretly.

3. d. South West England. The first cases were in Weymouth and Bristol, both ports that had ships arriving from Europe. The source of the plague was fleas from rats. It is estimated, within the following two years, about 30 to 40% of the British population were killed as a result. It killed similar numbers throughout Europe. The disease was brutal and death was fast. The Italian writer, Boccaccio, wrote that victims "ate lunch with their friends and dinner with their ancestors in paradise."

4. The Peasants' Revolt. He led an uprising from Kent in protest against a poll tax and restrictions on freedom.

He met Richard II in London, after the peasants had ransacked the city and was promised certain reforms. Things got ugly and Tyler was wounded. He was taken to a hospital but was found and decapitated. His head was displayed on London Bridge, and the King rescinded the promises he had made.

5. Saladin. The Sultan led the Muslim military campaign against the Crusader states in the Levant. King Richard's crusaders won battles, but did not manage to take Jerusalem from him.

6. b. Thomas the archer. Will Scarlet was Robin Hood's nephew. Little John was a big man who fought with Robin, with quarterstaves over a river and then became friends. Much the Miller's son helped rescue Robin from captivity.

7. Scotland. Robert Bruce led the Scots to victory against the English. The battle is unusual in that it lasted two days, whereas most medieval battles lasted only a day, at most. King Edward II fled to Dunbar Castle, and the only soldiers to escape were Welsh spearmen, who managed to get to Carlisle.

8. The Battle of Agincourt. It took place in Pas de Calais, France, on the 24th October 1415. Henry V's army had a large number of English and Welsh archers that used longbows to lethal effect, resulting in victory against the more numerous French.

9. Owain Glyndŵr. He led the revolt against Henry IV of England. He vanished and was never captured or betrayed, after the uprising was quelled, and died four years later.

10. William Caxton / Caxton. From Kent, he had moved to Bruges and after seeing printing presses in Cologne, started his own. The first book he printed was in 1473. He then set up a printing press in England and published The Canterbury Tales in 1476. Other books,

in English, he printed include the Bible and Aesop's Fables.

Tudor

1. b. 1st Cousin - 13 times removed. Queen Elizabeth II is directly related to all past kings and queens since 1714, when George I of Hanover, Germany became king of the United Kingdom. Prior to that not all are direct ancestors, however going back further they are. For example, King William the Conqueror of 1066 is her 22nd Grandfather, although hundreds of thousands of people are also descendants of him.

2. Mary Rose. The ship sank in 1545 during a battle with a French invasion fleet. There is now a dedicated museum in Portsmouth, where the preserved remains of the hull and artefacts can be viewed.

3. Leather & wool dealer. His father, John Shakespeare, sold gloves etc. William Shakespeare's grandfather, Richard Shakespeare, was a tenant farmer.

4. d. First English baby to be born in the American colonies. She was born in Roanoke Colony (now North Carolina), on 18th August 1587. Her parents were from London and her father was a bricklayer.

5. d. Playing bowls. During the sea battle he was aboard the ship, Revenge. In 1591 the ship was captured by the Spanish, then sunk in a huge storm off the Azores, west of Portugal.

6. a. 200,000. The population of London is now 8.6 million. Cities in the UK now that are a similar population size to Elizabethan London, include Bournemouth, Bath, Peterborough and Colchester.

7. The Babington Plot. Named after the chief conspirator, Anthony Babington. The plot was discovered by Queen Elizabeth's spymaster Sir Francis Walsingham. All those involved were executed, and

Queen Mary was beheaded; after Queen Elizabeth signed her death warrant.

8. a. Catherine of Aragon. He was married to her for 24 years, before divorce. She died whilst under arrest. The remaining five wives all followed in the space of a decade.

9. The Battle of Flodden. The battle took place on the England side of the border, and lasted about 3 hours. King James IV of Scotland, twelve Scottish earls, fourteen lords, one archbishop, three bishops and sixty-eight knights and gentlemen and an estimated 10,000 Scottish fighters were killed.

10. a. 9. Son of King Henry VIII and Jane Seymour. He was 9 when he became king in 1547, after his father died. A regency council governed, as he was too young. He died aged just 15 years old, after suffering from either T.B or pneumonia.

Stuart

1. Isaac Newton. He named the the seven colours of the spectrum, and explained his discoveries in public lectures between 1669 and 1671. Later, in 1704 his famous book, Opticks: or, A Treatise of the Reflexions, Refractions, Inflexions and Colours of Light was published.

2. d. Pudding Lane. The fire began in Thomas Farriner's bakery and quickly spread. After 3 days over 13,000 homes had been destroyed, as well as other buildings, such as old St Paul's Cathedral.

3. b. Navy Board. This government organisation administered the day to day operations of the Royal Navy. Pepys was Clerk of the Acts, and played a leading role in improving sailor's food and professional standards.

4. b. East Anglia. At the time of the English Civil war, was when he was busiest and is thought to be responsible for the deaths of hundreds of, mostly, women that were accused of witchcraft.

5. Roundheads. Many of the Parliamentarian supporters of Cromwell were Puritans and had short, close cropped hair. The term was seen as an insult at the time. The Cavalier royalists were more likely to have long hair and more flamboyant clothes.

6. Queen Anne. An English Baroque architectural style from her reign of 1702 - 1714. It was copied in the late Victorian and early Edwardian period, and this is known as Queen Anne Revival. Many of the red brick townhouses of Mayfair, London, from when the Duke of Westminster redeveloped the area in the late 1800s, are of this style.

7. War of the Three Kingdoms. The English Civil War was part of an intertwined series of conflicts that took place in England, Ireland, and Scotland between 1639 and 1651. The belligerents were the English Parliamentary Army, the Royalists, the Irish Confederates and the Scottish Covenanters.

8. d. Robert Catesby. All four were part of the plot. He was killed at Holbeche House after being surrounded by the Sheriff of Worcester and 200 armed men and his head was displayed at Parliament. John Wright was shot dead, as was Thomas Percy, who is said to have been killed by the same musket ball as Robert Catesby. Thomas Wintour, was Robert Catesby's cousin. He was shot in the arm and captured. He was then tortured in the Tower of London, and hanged, then drawn and quartered in early 1606.

9. b. Seed Drill. From Basildon in Berkshire, Tull invented a horse drawn seed drill that sowed the seeds in neat rows. This was one of the inventions that began a huge increase in food production and the start of

modern agriculture. Other inventions; reflecting telescope - James Gregory 1663 , pocket watch - Christiaan Huygens 1675 (Netherlands) , steam engine - Thomas Savery 1698

10. Anthony van Dyck / van Dyck. The British Royal Collection has 26 of his paintings, including portraits of the Royal Family. The National Gallery in London owns 14 paintings. His paintings are also on display in other galleries in Europe and the USA.

Georgian

1. a. Debt. Charles's father, John, was imprisoned for 3 months for debt, and managed to be released after Charles's grandma died and left the family £450 in her will.

2. d. Greece. He fought in the Greek War of Independence against the Ottoman Empire. He died there, aged 36, after contracting a fever.

3. Jane Austen. Born in Hampshire, the daughter of an Anglican rector, her famous books include Pride and Prejudice and Mansfield Park. Instead of her name, as author, it simply read 'By a Lady'. She is buried in Winchester Cathedral.

4. d. Brighton. It is unique for its Indian style architecture. Queen Victoria later sold it to the local council to fund Osborne House, her summer residence that was built on the Isle of Wight.

5. b. Robert Walpole. He was MP for Kings Lynn, then Earl of Orford from 1742.

6. The Whigs. The Tories were supported by the landed classes and Royal Family and the Whigs were supported by wealthy merchants and industrialists. Whigs supported extending the franchise, abolishing slavery, free trade and supremacy of Parliament over the monarch.

7. a. Seasickness. In a letter sent in October 1804 to Lord Camden, a year before the Battle of Trafalgar, Nelson wrote that he suffered from seasickness when there was strong winds.

8. The Battle of Waterloo. They were part of the victorious Seventh Coalition, Brunswick and Nassau made up the rest of the coalition. The battle took place in what is now modern-day Belgium, on the 18th June 1815, against France, that was led by Napoleon Bonaparte.

9. d. Hanover. King George I was made king of Britain after Queen Anne died, when he was 54. He was German and Anne's closest living Protestant relative. There was 54 Catholics that were closer blood relatives, but the Act of Settlement in 1701 banned them from inheriting the British throne.

10. d. Bath. It was designed by John Wood the Younger and built between 1767 and 1774. Number 1. Royal Crescent is owned by the Bath Preservation Trust and it is possible to visit and see what the townhouses were furnished like, when the street was first built.

Victorian

1. c. 81. She died in 1901, at Osborne House, Isle of Wight.

2. d. Lady with the Lamp. From a report in The Times. She was given the name due to her doing solitary rounds of the hospital at night, to check on injured soldiers.

3. a. Electrochemistry. He had little formal education, but discovered the principles underlying electromagnetic induction, diamagnetism and electrolysis.

4. d. Preston North End. They also won the FA Cup that season, making them the first ever league and cup

double winners. They won with 40 points. Aston Villa came second with 29 points, Everton came eighth with 20 points and Notts County came eleventh with 12 points.

5. d. Vacuum traction. He used Clegg and Samuda's patented system of atmospheric (vacuum) traction, whereby stationary pumps sucked air from a pipe placed in the centre of the railway track. The trains reached speeds of up to 68mph. However, there was various problems that made it more expensive than conventional steam power, so the project was ended.

6. a. 4 and 5. Thousands of under 13 year olds were found to be working in mines throughout the UK, with some of the youngest being just 4 and 5 years old and others that had started at that age, but were older at the time of the report.

7. a. Telephone. He was born in Edinburgh and moved to Canada and was just 29 years old when he received the patent for a device 'to transmit vocal or other sounds telegraphically'.

8. d. Potatoes. One third of the population relied on potatoes as their main food source. Blight created a massive shortage, which resulted in an estimated 1 million deaths and 1 million emigrating during the famine.

9. d. Newcastle upon Tyne. Mosley Street was lit by Joseph Swan's incandescent lamp on 3 February 1879.

10. a. Beagle. His third voyage between 1837 and 1843 was during the reign of Queen Victoria. It explored the coastline of Australia.

Edwardian

1. b. Belfast. It was built at the Harland & Wolff shipyard and sank on her maiden voyage, from Southampton, sailing to New York on 15th April 1912.

The ship hit an iceberg. Thomas Andrews, the naval architect that designed the ship, was one of the victims.

2. d. Liberals. Led by Henry Campbell - Bannerman, they won 397 seats, an increase of 214 from the previous General Election. They defeated the governing Conservatives, led by Arthur Balfour. The Tories lost 246 seats, including Balfour's seat of Manchester East.

3. Emily Davison. She stepped in front of King George V's horse, Anmer, at the Epsom Derby on June the 4th, 1913. Seriously injured, she died a few days later. Prior to this protest she had been heavily involved in the Suffragette movement and was imprisoned nine times. On the night of the 1911 Census she hid in a cupboard in the House of Commons, so she could write it was her place of residence. The other 3 choices, were also leading Suffragettes.

4. d. Glasgow. He was born in the city and designed the Glasgow School of Art building, which is considered to be the masterpiece of his career.

5. a. Flew across the English Channel. Frenchman, Louis Bleriot was the first ever person to fly across the English Channel in an aeroplane. The Daily Mail had set a challenge, and offered £1000 to the first person to do so. He flew from Calais, early in the morning, on the 25th July, 1909, and travelled at a speed of 45mph, at an altitude of about 250 feet. 36 minutes and 30 seconds later, he landed near Dover Castle, Kent. He won the prize and became world famous.

6. Peter Pan. The play was performed at the Duke of York's Theatre, London. A novel was later published in 1911.

7. Edward Elgar. One of his most famous tunes is 'Nimrod' from Enigma Variations, which is played every year during the Remembrance Sunday ceremony at the Cenotaph in London.

8. d. VII (7th). He was the eldest son of Queen Victoria and was king from 1901 until 1910.

9. Great Britain. They won 56 gold medals. United States, second with 23 golds. Sweden, third with 8 golds and France came fourth, winning five golds. A total of 22 nations took part.

10. b. Irish Parliamentary Party. At that time there was MPs from the whole of Ireland in the House of Commons. Their leader, John Richmond, was MP for Waterford City. The party won 74 seats. Conservatives came second with 271 seats, just 1 less than the Liberals. The Liberals formed a government with the backing of the Irish nationalists. Labour, a growing, young party, came fourth with 42 seats. Social Democratic Coalition, was a far left party and only stood in two seats and won neither.

World War One

1. d. 19,200. Including the injured, the British casualties were 57,470 in just the first 24 hours of the battle, which lasted until the 18th November, 1916.

2. Agatha Christie. She was a Red Cross nurse at a hospital in Torquay, from 1914 to 1918, and became a dispenser of medicine in 1917. In WW2 she volunteered as a dispenser in the dispensary of University College Hospital in London. At the time many medicines were prepared by hand and her knowledge of poisons later helped her when she was writing murder mystery novels.

3. a. John McCrae. He wrote it in 1915, whilst serving in the Canadian Expeditionary Force, after a friend was killed. It was first published in Punch magazine, later that year. McCrae died in France in 1918, after an illness. Wilfred Owen was killed in action one week before the end of the war. He was posthumously awarded the Military Cross for gallantry on 1st/2nd

October 1918. Siegfried Sassoon survived the war and died in 1967, aged 80. Rupert Brooke died in 1915, after falling ill on a ship, whilst sailing to land at Gallipoli. He was buried in an olive grove on the Greek island, Skyros.

4. Herbert Henry Asquith / H.H Asquith / Asquith. He was a Liberal and Prime Minister between 1908 and 1916. David Lloyd George succeeded him. His eldest son, Raymond was killed in action, during the Battle of the Somme.

5. Royal Flying Corps. It merged with the Royal Naval Air Service to create a new section of the Armed Forces dedicated to air warfare. However, in later years, the Royal Navy and Army both regained their own aviation sections, the Fleet Air Arm (Royal Navy) and the Army Air Corps (British Army).

6. d. Killed when the ship he was on hit a mine. He was aboard HMS Hampshire, travelling to Russia for talks, when it hit a German mine west of the Orkney Islands, on the 5th June 1916. 737 aboard the ship were killed, with just 12 survivors.

7. Harry Patch. He died in 2009, aged 111. During the war he was an assistant gunner in the Duke of Cornwall's Light Infantry and was injured at the Battle of Passchendaele, after a shell exploded, that killed his three friends.

8. Zeppelin/s. Named after German Count Ferdinand von Zeppelin. They travelled about 85 m.p.h and could carry 2 tons of bombs. The first raid in 1915 was on Great Yarmouth and King's Lynn. In total the Zeppelin raids killed 557 people.

9. Great Britain. 6,094 British sailors were killed. The German Navy lost 2,551 men. A total of 250 war ships took part in the battle, off the coast of Denmark.

10. a. Alec Douglas-Home. Born in 1903, he was still a boy during the war. Harold McMillan was a Captain in the Grenadier Guards and fought in the Battle of Loos and the Battle of the Somme. He was badly injured and spent the last two years of the war in hospital. Clement Atlee ended the war as a Major, and had fought at Gallipoli and in the Middle East. Anthony Eden was a commissioned officer in a battalion of the King's Royal Rifle Corps, and served on the Western Front in France. He was awarded the Military Cross. His older and younger brother were both killed during the war.

Interwar

1. d. Ramsey McDonald. Born in Lossiemouth, Scotland, 1866.

2. d. Pass the driving test. Since then more than 46 million UK citizens have passed the test.

3. Alexander Fleming. In 1928, while researching influenza, Fleming noticed that mould had developed accidentally on a set of culture dishes being used to grow the staphylococci germ. The mould had made a bacteria-free circle around itself. After further research he named the substance Penicillin. In 1945 he was awarded the Nobel Prize for Medicine.

4. BBC Television began its scheduled broadcasting. At first the viewer numbers were in the hundreds. In 1937 it did its first coverage of Wimbledon Tennis. The television service was suspended during the war. It was feared VHF transmissions could help the Luftwaffe target central London, and many of the technical staff were needed to work on Radar defences.

5. d. Jarrow. Approximately, two hundred men were selected from the Tyneside town to take part, and they set off on the 291 mile march on the 5th October, arriving in London on the 31st October. On the 4th November the town's petition, with 11,000 signatures,

asking that "His Majesty's Government and this honourable House should realise the urgent need that work should be provided for the town without further delay", was presented to the House of Commons by Jarrow MP Ellen Wilkinson. The closure of Palmer's shipyard in the town, its main employer, had caused mass unemployment.

6. a. Australia. She left Britain on the 5th May and crash landed in Darwin, 11,000 miles later, on the 24th May. The de Havilland Gipsy Moth, she flew, can be viewed at the Science Museum in London. During WWII, Amy Johnson served in the Air Transport Auxiliary and died after the plane she was flying crashed into the River Thames. Amelia Earhart, from Kansas was the first female pilot to cross the Atlantic, in 1932. She departed from Newfoundland and landed in Northern Ireland. In 1912, Harriet Quimby, an American aviator was the first female to fly across the English Channel to France.

7. c. Three times. Consecutively - 1934, 1935, 1936. He also won the U.S Championships three times (1933, 1934, 1936), and the Australian Championships (1934) and French Championships (1935).

8. Charlie Chaplin. He was born in South London and grew up in the city, before moving to America to embark on his renowned Hollywood movie career. The Kid was a silent movie that lasted 68 minutes. It cost $250,000 to make and made $5.4 million at the box office.

9. Oswald Mosley. After serving as an officer in the 16th Queen's Lancers, then as an observer in the Royal Flying Corp, during WW1 (2nd Battle of Ypres and Battle of Loos), he became Conservative MP for Harrow, at the age of just 21. Disagreeing with their use of the 'Black & Tans' in Ireland, he became independent. He then later became a Labour MP for Smethwick. As Chancellor of the Duchy of Lancaster in

the Labour Government, he was tasked with reducing unemployment. His radical proposals were rejected, which led to him leaving the party and starting the New Party, which merged to become the B.U.F in 1932.

10. b. Albert. His full name was Albert Frederick Arthur George, and was named after his great grandfather, Albert, husband of Queen Victoria, who was still alive when he was born in 1895.

Empire

1. b. Motorbike accident. He was killed, aged 46, in 1935, when he swerved to avoid two children on their bikes, after coming up from a dip in the road near Wareham in Dorset.

2. b. 1901. It became a fully independent, self-governing nation within the British Empire on the 1st January, 1901.

3. d. British Honduras. It became a crown colony in 1862, a self-governing colony in 1964, was renamed in 1973 and became fully independent in 1981.

4. b. Shimla. The city was created in the dense forests of the Himalayas, as a place to escape the scorching summer heat. Many fine buildings from the era remain, including the Neo-Gothic, Christ Church.

5. c. 23.8%. A total of 35.5 million square kilometres / 13.7 million square miles.

6. a. Pitcairn Islands. The population is about 49 people, who reside on Pitcairn, the second largest of 4 small volcanic islands. Total land area - 18 square miles.

7. c. Botswana. CAF was made up of Southern Rhodesia (Zimbabwe), Northern Rhodesia (Zambia), and Nyasaland (Malawi). Botswana was formerly the British protectorate of Bechuanaland and became independent Botswana in 1966.

8. They are all named after Queen Victoria. Victoria Falls / Mosi-oa-Tunya on the river Zambezi Zambia/Zimbabwe. 108 metres / 354 feet in height. Lake Victoria, Uganda, Kenya, Tanzania border. 337 km / 209.4 miles in length. Mount Victoria, near Wellington. 196 metres / 643 feet high, 4 miles north of Mount Albert. The city of Victoria, Canada. Capital of British Columbia, approximate 80,000 population.

9. Raffles Hotel. Sir Thomas Stamford Raffles (1781 – 1826) founded Singapore in 1819. Raffles Hotel opened in 1887.

10. a. Kenya. They lived around the town of Nyeri, close to the Aberdare mountains. By 1939 there was 21,000 white British living in Kenya.

World War Two

1. c. St Michael's - Coventry. On the night of the 14th November 1940, Coventry suffered a massive attack by 515 Luftwaffe bombers. 568 people were killed and thousands of homes and factories were destroyed. The cathedral was hit by incendiary devices from 8pm onwards and was utterly destroyed in a firestorm. A cross of burnt timbers was discovered in the ruins. The cross can be viewed in the modern cathedral built alongside the ruins, after the war. Outside, in the roofless ruins there is a replica cross with the words FATHER FORGIVE alongside it.

2. a. Norway. A total of 38,000 Allied soldiers from Britain, France and Poland, tried to help the Norwegian army, but were unable to stop the German invasion. The Norwegian King, King Haakon, Crown Prince Olav and Norway's government managed to escape to Britain on HMS Glasgow and remained in exile for the duration of the war. Norwegian pilots, soldiers and sailors that managed to escape, fought for the Allies.

For example two RAF Spitfire squadrons, 331 and 332 were mostly Norwegian pilots.

3. Bletchley Park. At its peak the code breaking centre had 10,000 staff, three quarters of which were women. Many of the staff were skilled in languages, maths, physics or engineering. Alan Turing, who led hut 8, played a pivotal role in cracking intercepted naval Enigma coded messages. It was not until the 1970s that the general public began to learn of the secret & vital work that took place at Bletchley.

4. Home Guard. Initially called Local Defence Volunteers, it was set up to defend Britain from invasion, made up of men to old or young to join the armed forces and men in reserved occupations, that were essential to the war effort, eg. munitions workers. A total of 1,206 were killed in air attacks whilst on duty. For bravery, two members of the Home Guard were posthumously awarded the George Cross, 13 were awarded the George Medal, one was mentioned in dispatches and 58 were awarded the King's Commendation for Brave Conduct.

5. d. Gold. Omaha and Utah were beaches that U.S forces landed on. Juno was the beach the Canadians landed on. British troops landed on Gold beach. They also landed on Sword beach. Airborne units landed behind enemy lines in the hours before the beach landings. Approximately 156,000 Allied soldiers took part in the invasion of the coast of Normandy, France.

6. d. No legs. He was a double amputee, due to being in a plane crash in December 1931, after he joined the RAF in 1928. Discharged in 1933 he re-joined the RAF when WWII began and became an ace fighter pilot, flying a Spitfire during the Battle of Britain. In 1941 he crashed in France and was taken prisoner and was held captive at Colditz Castle until 1945.

7. HMS Hood. 1,416 men out of a total crew of 1,419 died after a direct hit penetrated the deck and exploded in one of the ship's magazines, where the ammunition was stored. Midshipman William Dundas, Able Seaman Bob Tilburn and Ordinary Signalman Ted Briggs were the three survivors. William Dundas died after a car crash aged 42. Both Bob Tilburn and Ted Briggs lived until old age. Ted Briggs was the last living survivor and died age 85 in 2008.

8. d. An airman that parachuted or crash landed into the sea. At the end of the war, the club had a total of 9000 members from Allied forces, all of which whose lives were saved by a life jacket, inflatable dinghy, or similar device. Another club, the Caterpillar Club was for all those that had bailed out of a damaged plane hit by enemy fire or a failing engine, using a parachute, but included those that had landed on the ground.

9. SAS. Their first mission in November 1941, a parachute drop, was considered a disaster with at least 22, a third of the initial group, either killed or captured. Its second raid was a great success, destroying many enemy aircraft at three Libyan airfields. David Stirling was taken POW in 1943 and was sent to Colditz Castle.

10. Barnes Wallis. (1887 - 1979). His 'bouncing bombs' were used with devastating effect on the dams of the Ruhr Valley. Two hydroelectric power stations were destroyed, and approximately 1600 civilians drowned, as a result of flooding, when the bombs that skimmed the reservoirs exploded the dam walls. He also invented a Geodetic airframe that was used in Wellington bombers.

Post War

1. Aneurin Bevan / Bevan. (1897 - 1960). Son of a miner, he was M.P for Ebbw Vale, in Wales. The NHS was launched on 5 July 1948, offering free diagnosis

and treatment for all. He resigned from the government in 1951 in protest against the introduction of prescription charges for spectacles and dental treatment.

2. MV Empire Windrush / Empire Windrush / Windrush. The ship was a German troopship during WWII, under the name Monte Rosa. It was seized by the UK at the end of the war. The British Nationality Act 1948 gave all people living in the Commonwealth full rights of entry and settlement in Britain. Legislation to control immigration was made in 1962, but it still continued. According to the BBC 'In 1945, Britain's non-white residents numbered in the low thousands.' By the 2011 Census the non white population was more than 7 million.

3. c. Portugal. They beat them 2-1. The other two teams were in the same group as England. Mexico were eliminated and Uruguay got beat 4-0 in the Quarter Finals.

4. b. Remain a member of the European Community. The UK joined on January 1, 1973 under the Conservative government of Edward Heath. The Labour Party pledged to hold a referendum on the issue, and they won the 1974 General Election.

5. c. Kenya. Princess Elizabeth was staying at the Tree Tops Hotel, in Aberdare National Park and she was later informed of the news at Sagana Lodge.

6. c. 1,354 mph. It flew at twice the speed of sound. The supersonic jet was a joint enterprise with France, and began commercial flights in 1976, and could carry up to 128 passengers. Concorde flew from Paris and London to the USA for the next 27 years. On average a flight from London to New York took 3 hours 30 minutes. Its fastest ever transatlantic crossing was on 7th February 1996, when it flew from New York to London in just 2 hours 52 minutes. The average flight

time for the same journey, on a jumbo jet, is 6 hours 40 minutes to 7 hours.

7. The Troubles. A total of 3,532 people were killed, including 1,049 Royal Ulster Constabulary and British Armed Forces personnel, and 1,841 civilians. More than 47,000 people were injured.

8. c. Stevenage. Population - approx. 85,000. It was the first new town, of a total of 22, designated to be built, in 1946 and in the years that followed, to address the housing shortage following World War Two. All four towns are in the county of Herefordshire, that borders north London. Hertford is the county town, and has existed since before the Domesday Book of 1086. Letchworth was the first 'Garden City' created in 1905. Welwyn Garden City was the second, built in the 1920s.

9. a. Silver Beatles. Prior to that they were known as The Quarrymen, named after Quarry Bank School, that Paul McCartney and John Lennon had attended.

10. c. Iran. On the 5th May 1980, live on national TV, the SAS stormed the Iranian Embassy, overlooking Hyde Park in London. In just 17 minutes they rescued 19 hostages and kill five of the six terrorists. One hostage was killed in the crossfire. The hostage crisis had begun on the 30th April, when Arab separatists, from a region of Iran stormed into the embassy with machine guns and started demanding concessions. Soon after they had killed one of the hostages and pushed the body out the front door, on the 5th May, and threatened more to follow. Prime Minister Margaret Thatcher gave the go ahead to the SAS to end the siege. They abseiled from the roof, and entered after exploding the window.

Who Said What

1. a. Admiral Nelson. A flag signal was sent to the fleet by Vice Admiral Horatio Nelson, from his flagship

HMS Victory, as the Battle of Trafalgar was about to commence on 21 October 1805. Popham's "Telegraphic Signals of Marine Vocabulary" was used.

2. c. Queen Elizabeth. In a speech delivered by Queen Elizabeth to her troops who were assembled at Tilbury Camp to defend the country against a Spanish invasion in 1588.

3. b. Henry Morton Stanley. Stanley, a Welsh born American journalist, found Livingstone on 10 November 1871 in Ujiji, near Lake Tanganyika in what is now the nation of Tanzania. Livingstone had lost contact with the outside world for 6 years.

4. d. David Lloyd George. He visited Hitler in the 1930s and was quoted in The Post, 23rd September, 1936.

5. a. Queen Victoria. 1870.

6. b. King Edward VIII, announcing his abdication as King in 1936.

7. d. Winston Churchill.

8. a. George Orwell

9. d. William Wilberforce MP. Slavery abolitionist. In 1833 the government passed a bill that banned slavery in the British Empire.

10. Princess Diana

ALSO AVAILABLE

World War 2 Quiz - H.C Dilston

Quiz sections - Dunkirk, Battle of Britain, The Blitz, The War at Sea, Raf Bomber Command, The Desert, Occupied Europe, Eastern Front, Sicily & Italy, Hitler & the Nazis, Who Said What, D-Day and the Advance on Germany, War Against Japan, Persecution, Tanks & Weapons.

ISBN - 978-1326421298

Printed in Great Britain
by Amazon